Favo
CHRISTMAS

T R E A T S

*The second Christmas treats book,
with fabulous family banquets, wicked
treats, home-made goodies from the gourmet
pantry and creative craft ideas
for presents*

KÖNEMANN

CONTENTS

*I*t's on again — the Christmas season,
with its excitement and frustration, rewards,
demands and triumphs.
Favourite Christmas Treats *offers a new selection of reliably
delicious foods: banquet-style spreads to feed the family,
wicked treats you've perhaps waited all year to enjoy (and
then again, perhaps not), and a special collection of gourmet
goodies for yourself or someone you love.
Creative craft ideas for attractive home-made gifts that won't
break the budget range from simple paper Christmas
bonbons to bright paper-covered boxes children can make,
and elegant wreaths for your own or someone else's front
door or living room.
This is a Christmas book packed with ideas,
to read many times and enjoy.*

Festive Spreads

Roast Turkey, the centrepiece of a Christmas banquet

*T*his chapter offers two Christmas banquets. One presents Roast Turkey with Cranberry and Apricot Stuffing as the centrepiece and is served with a selection of delectable and nutritious vegetable dishes. Not all of these may be required on the day; you can choose among the recipes according to taste and the number of people you expect to entertain.

The second banquet is ideal for those who would prefer a do-ahead cold collation.

It features a seafood platter which in itself involves very little preparation and is open to improvisation. This is served with an array of sauces and other delicious accompaniments.

Roast Turkey with Cranberry and Apricot Stuffing

Preparation time:
  15 minutes
Cooking time:
  3 hours
Serves 10
✳

1 × 5.5 kg turkey
30 g butter, melted
1 tablespoon oil

STUFFING
3 cups fresh
  breadcrumbs
½ cup chopped dried
  apricots
½ cup cranberry sauce
1/3 cup slivered
  almonds, toasted
1 onion, finely
  chopped
rind and juice ½ lemon
2 tablespoons chopped
  fresh parsley
1 egg, beaten
¼ teaspoon mixed
  herbs
salt and pepper

1 If your turkey is frozen, make sure that

1

Roast Turkey with all the trimmings

1 *To carve turkey, place bird breast-side up on a chopping board. Using a sharp knife, slice through skin between breast and thigh. Pull back leg to locate joint. Cut through joint. Remove wing in the same manner, cutting through skin at corner of breast around wing.*
2 *Separate drumstick and thigh by cutting through centre joint.*
3 *Carve the drumstick by placing the knife parallel to the bone. Slice horizontally.*
4 *Carve thigh by slicing parallel to the bone. Carve breast by cutting diagonally to produce thin slices. Use the back of carving fork to avoid piercing meat.*

it is thoroughly thawed before proceeding. Wash inside and out. Dry with kitchen paper.
2 To prepare stuffing, combine all ingredients well.
3 Spoon prepared stuffing into cavity. Cover with neck flap. Secure with wing tips or a skewer. Tie legs together.

4 Place turkey on a trivet in a large baking dish. Brush with combined butter and oil. Pour about 4 cm of water into dish.
5 Brush a large piece of foil with a little of the butter mixture. Cover turkey loosely with foil, ensuring a tight seal around rim of dish.
6 Bake at 220°C for 3

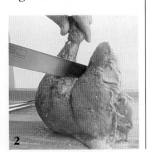

2

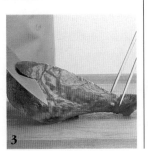

3

4

hours. Remove foil for the last 30 minutes to allow it to brown.

7 To test if turkey is cooked, insert a skewer into the thigh. If the juices that come away are clear, the bird is ready. If they are still pink, continue cooking for a little longer.

8 Transfer turkey to a serving platter. Cover with foil to keep warm whilst resting. Retain pan juices for gravy (see recipe). Serve with gravy, cranberry sauce and vegetables.

Gravy

Preparation time:
  5 minutes
Cooking time:
  3 minutes
Makes about 2 cups
✳

2 tablespoons plain flour
¼ cup sweet sherry
reserved pan juices
turkey or chicken stock (see *Note*)
salt and pepper

1 Whisk flour and sherry together to make a smooth paste.
2 Make pan juices up to 2½ cups with stock. Blend into flour mixture.
3 Transfer to a saucepan. Cook over high heat, stirring constantly, until mixture boils and thickens. Simmer for 3 minutes. Season to taste.

Note: Use chicken stock cubes or make fresh stock by simmering turkey giblets in 1 litre water with flavourings for about 1 hour. Strain.

Parmesan Potatoes

Preparation time:
  10 minutes
Cooking time:
  1 hour
Serves 10
✳

20 medium-sized potatoes, peeled
2 teaspoons salt
60 g butter, melted
¼ cup grated Parmesan cheese
2 tablespoons dry breadcrumbs

1 Slice potatoes at 5 mm intervals through the centre (make sure you do not cut all the way through — they should hang together at the bottom).

2 Place potatoes cut side up in a greased baking pan. Sprinkle with salt. Brush with melted butter.

3 Bake at 220°C for about 45 minutes or until potatoes are tender, brushing occasionally with butter.

4 Sprinkle with combined Parmesan and breadcrumbs. Bake for a further 10–15 minutes.

Creamy Carrots

Preparation time:
  10 minutes
Cooking time:
  10 minutes*
Serves 10
✳

5 carrots, cleaned
30 g butter
2 tablespoons brown sugar
½ cup cream
2 tablespoons chopped chives

1 Cut carrots into sticks or rings. Cook in simmering water until just tender Drain.
2 Melt butter in the same pan. Add sugar. Cook 1 minute. Pour in cream. Bring to the boil.

3 Reduce heat. Return carrots to pan and toss well. Serve, sprinkled with chives.

Minted Peas

Preparation time:
   nil
Cooking time:
   6 minutes
Serves 10
✳

3 cups fresh or frozen
   peas
few sprigs mint
2 tablespoons chopped
   fresh mint

1 Cook peas in simmering water with mint sprigs until tender. Drain.
2 Return to pan. Toss in chopped fresh mint and serve.

Baked Stuffed Onions

Preparation time:
   10 minutes
Cooking time:
   35 minutes
Serves 10
✳

10 onions, peeled
½ cup fresh
   breadcrumbs
½ cup grated Cheddar
1 tomato, peeled and
   chopped

¼ teaspoon dried basil
seasonings to taste

1 Cook onions in simmering water for 5 minutes or until just tender then drain.
2 Using a small pointed knife, remove the centre core.
3 Combine all remaining ingredients. Fill each cavity with the stuffing.
4 Brush a baking dish with oil. Add onions. Bake at 220°C for 30 minutes.

Baked Pumpkin

Preparation time:
   5 minutes
Cooking time:
   50 minutes
Serves 10
✳

10 chunks pumpkin,
   retain skin
oil

1 Cook pumpkin in simmering water for 5

minutes or until just tender then drain.
2 Place enough oil in a baking pan to just cover the base. Add pumpkin. Bake at 220°C for about 45 minutes, basting occasionally. Turn halfway through cooking. Drain pumpkin on kitchen paper before serving.

VARIATION
Once turned, spread top surface of pumpkin with a paste of 2 cloves garlic, crushed, and 1 teaspoon powdered ginger. Continue as directed, basting occasionally.

Garlic Asparagus

Preparation time:
   5 minutes
Cooking time:
   5 minutes
Serves 10
✳

1 bunch asparagus
30 g butter
1 clove garlic, crushed
seasoning to taste

1 Slice asparagus into 2.5 cm lengths on the diagonal.
2 Melt butter in a frying pan. Add garlic, seasonings and asparagus. Stir-fry until

asparagus is just tender and serve immediately.

Note: Beans may be substituted for asparagus.

Mushroom Roll-ups

Preparation time:
  5 minutes
Cooking time:
  30 minutes
Makes 15
✳

**5 rashers rindless
  bacon
15 button mushrooms
toothpicks**

1 Cut each rasher of bacon in half. Cut the large end of each rasher into 2, lengthways. You will now have 3 thin strips of bacon.
2 Wrap a strip of bacon around each mushroom. Secure with toothpicks. Place in an ovenproof dish.

3 Bake at 220°C for about 30 minutes. Allow 1–2 per person.

Bubbly Fruit Cocktail

Preparation time:
  10 minutes
Cooking time:
  nil
*Makes about 1 cup fruit
  purée*
✳

**1 punnet strawberries,
  washed and hulled
4 peaches, peeled and
  stones removed (see
  Note)
2 tablespoons fresh
  mint, roughly
  chopped
1 tablespoon brandy
1 tablespoon brown
  sugar (optional)
ice-cold champagne
fresh mint leaves**

1 Place all ingredients except champagne and

mint leaves in a food processor or blender. Process until smooth.
2 Spoon 2 teaspoons of purée into champagne glasses. Pour in some champagne. Mix with a swizzle stick. Garnish with mint leaves.

Note: 1 × 425 g can sliced peaches, drained, may be used in place of fresh peaches.

Salmon Dip

Preparation time:
  10 minutes
Cooking time:
  nil
Makes about 3½ cups
✳

**1 × 400 g can pink
  salmon, drained
1 × 250 g packet cream
  cheese, softened
½ cup prepared
  mayonnaise
¼ cup sour cream
juice of 1 lemon
3-4 gherkins, chopped
1 tablespoon chopped
  chives
freshly ground black
  pepper**

1 Place all ingredients in a food processor or blender. Process until smooth.
2 Transfer to a serving dish. Refrigerate until required. Serve with crackers.

H I N T S

- Make fresh breadcrumbs by processing stale bread until fine crumbs are achieved. Plan ahead and freeze crumbs.
- Frozen turkeys are best defrosted slowly in the refrigerator. This may take 24 hours.
- Serve a light red wine with your turkey or a dry white. A sweeter dessert wine or champagne is lovely served with sweets.
- Why not serve all accompaniments in a buffet style?

Bubbly Fruit Cocktail and Salmon Dip

Clockwise from top rear:
Refreshing Green Salad,
Spicy Stuffed Ham, Pistachio
Sauce, Dill Mustard Sauce,
Asparagus Cheese Rolls,
Seafood Platter, Mini Cheese
Balls with fresh grapes and
Cranberry Borscht

Seafood Platter

Preparation time:
   10 minutes
Cooking time:
   nil
Serves 8-10
✳

**3-4 kg fresh cooked
   prawns**
**4 fresh cooked crab or
   lobster**
**6 dozen fresh oysters
   in the shell**

1 The day before
Christmas, go down to
your local fish market
and inspect the produce
on display. The
ingredients we have
given here are just
suggestions. Add or
subtract your favourite
fruits of the sea for a
splendid banquet with
minimal preparation.
Other suggestions are: a
whole salmon poached
in water and dry white
wine, with onions,
bayleaf and parsley;
barbecued fish steaks;
octopus salad.
2 Serve with Pistachio
Sauce and Dill Mustard
Sauce (see recipes).

13

Cranberry Borscht

Preparation time:
   5 minutes
Cooking time:
   10 minutes
Serves 8-10
✳

2 × 290 g jars cranberry
   sauce
2 × 430 g cans beef
   consommé
1 soup can water or to
   taste
1/3 cup lemon juice
lemon slices to
   decorate (optional)

1 In a saucepan,
combine cranberry
sauce, consommé, water
and lemon juice. Heat
to serving temperature,
stirring to blend well.
2 Serve garnished with
lemon slices, if desired.
Soup can be chilled and
served cold, if desired.

Dill Mustard Sauce

Preparation time:
   5 minutes plus
chilling
Cooking time:
   nil
Makes about 1 cup
✳

1/3 cup sugar
1-2 tablespoons dry
   mustard

3 teaspoons white
   vinegar
1½ tablespoons
   vegetable oil
½ cup sour cream
2 tablespoons chopped
   fresh dill (or 2
   teaspoons dried)

1 In a bowl stir together
sugar and mustard. Add
vinegar, then oil,
stirring well after each
until blended. Beat
vigorously until slightly
thickened.
2 Fold in sour cream
and dill. Cover and chill
several hours to let
flavours mellow. Serve
cold or at room
temperature.

Note: This sauce should
be quite tart to accent
the delicacy of the cold
seafood. Serve with
lobster, prawns, oysters
and mussels.

Mini Cheese Balls

Preparation time:
   10 minutes
Cooking time:
   nil
Makes about 15
✳

175 g Philadelphia
   cream cheese
¼ cup grated Gruyère
   cheese

¼ cup freshly grated
   Parmesan cheese
pinch dry mustard
salt and black pepper
pinch cayenne pepper
4-6 tablespoons finely
   chopped parsley or
   chervil

1 Beat the cream cheese
until smooth, then beat
in the two grated
cheeses. Add mustard,
salt, pepper and
cayenne pepper and mix
well.
2 Spoon the mixture
into a bowl, cover and
chill for 2 hours or until
firm.
3 Form the cheese into
small balls and roll each
one in chopped herbs.
Serve with crackers and
fresh fruit.

Spicy Stuffed Ham

Preparation time:
   30 minutes
Cooking time:
   1½-2 hours
Serves 10-12
✳✳

4 kg leg of ham, boned
   (see *Note*)
1 onion, chopped
2 cloves garlic,
   chopped
1 cup dry breadcrumbs
1/3 cup chopped fresh
   parsley
1 small red capsicum,

seeded and finely
chopped
2 eggs
1 tablespoon French
mustard
½ teaspoon pepper
1 cup bottled tomato
pasta sauce
2 cups dry red wine,
fruit juice, or
combination of both

ONION SAUCE
2 tablespoons chopped
onion
1 tablespoon butter
1 tablespoon plain
flour

1 With a sharp knife,
enlarge space where
ham bone has been
removed by cutting a
tunnel through length
of ham about 10 cm in
diameter, and removing
meat in pieces.
2 Coarsely grind ham
pieces in 2 batches in a
food processor with the
onion and garlic;
transfer to a large bowl.
3 Stir in breadcrumbs,
parsley, capsicum, eggs,
mustard and pepper and
mix well. Gently press
mixture back into centre
of ham. Tie ham
securely into shape with
kitchen string at 5 cm
intervals.
4 Place ham in a baking
tin. Score fat into a
diamond pattern with a
sharp knife, if desired.
Spread with tomato

sauce. Pour wine or
juice over and around
ham. Bake at 180°C for
1½ hours, basting
frequently with pan
juices after the first 30
minutes to glaze. Place
ham on a serving
platter. Cover and keep
warm.
5 To make onion sauce,
in a saucepan, cook
onion in butter until
tender. Stir in flour
until smooth. Add pan
juices, whisking until
smooth. Cook, stirring,
until thickened and
bubbly. (If too thick,
thin with extra wine or
fruit juice.) Slice ham
and serve with the
onion sauce poured over
or separately in a sauce
boat.

Note: Ask the butcher
to bone the leg and
remove the rind,
leaving fat layer intact.
Tie leg back into shape
to make Step 1 easier.

Asparagus Cheese Rolls

Preparation time:
  30 minutes
Cooking time:
  3-5 minutes
Makes 36-40
✳

18-20 slices white
  sandwich bread
125 g packet cream
  cheese, softened
125 g blue vein cheese,
  softened
1 egg yolk
¼ teaspoon
  Worcestershire sauce
pepper
340 g can asparagus
  spears, drained
melted butter

1 Trim crusts from
bread; cut lengthways in
half. Cover with a
dampened cloth and set
aside.
2 Beat together cream
and blue vein cheeses,
egg yolk, Worcester-
shire sauce and pepper
until smooth and fluffy.
3 Cut asparagus spears
crossways into pieces
long enough to fit the
width of bread fingers.
Spread cheese mixture
evenly over bread; top
each with an asparagus
piece and roll into
cylinders. Pinch ends
tightly to seal.
4 Arrange rolls on a
baking tray; brush tops

with melted butter. Cover with plastic film and chill or freeze until needed.

5 To serve, thaw, if frozen, then grill rolls about 12 cm from heat, turning occasionally, for 3–5 minutes until golden. Serve warm.

Pistachio Sauce

Preparation time:
  15 minutes
Cooking time:
  nil
Makes 1¾ cups
*

4-6 fresh young spinach leaves, washed and coarsely chopped
1 tablespoon chopped chives
⅓ cup peeled and coarsely chopped pistachio nuts
1½ cups homemade or purchased mayonnaise
pepper

1 In a blender or food processor, combine spinach leaves, chives and nuts. Add about 2 tablespoons of the mayonnaise and blend or process until finely chopped.
2 Transfer mixture to a bowl and stir in remaining mayonnaise. Season to taste. Serve chilled with seafood.

Refreshing Green Salad

Preparation time:
  40 minutes
Cooking time:
  nil
Makes 8-10 small servings
*

250-375 g fresh green beans, trimmed
1 head mignonette lettuce
1 ripe honeydew or rockmelon
2 firm ripe avocados
lemon juice
cherry tomatoes and spring onions to decorate (optional)

THYME MAYONNAISE
1 egg yolk
2 teaspoons grainy mustard
1 tablespoon white or red wine vinegar
pepper
¼ teaspoon sugar, or to taste
½ cup olive or vegetable oil
chopped fresh or dried thyme leaves

1 String beans, cut each in half lengthways or leave whole, if desired. Steam over simmering water, covered, until crisp-tender; drain and rinse under cold water. Drain, cover and chill.
2 To make mayonnaise, in a small bowl, whisk together egg yolk, mustard and vinegar with pepper and sugar to taste. Gradually add oil, whisking constantly, until smooth and thickened. Stir in thyme. Cover and chill.
3 To serve, arrange washed lettuce leaves on a large serving platter. Slice melon and avocados into thin wedges, removing seeds and rinds. Arrange with beans in separate rows over lettuce. Sprinkle avocado with a little lemon juice to prevent any discolouration.
4 Decorate platter with tomatoes and spring onions if desired. Serve with the thyme mayonnaise.

Tropical Chicken Salad with Raspberry Vinaigrette

Preparation time:
  20 minutes
Cooking time
  nil
Serves 4-6
*

1 mignonette lettuce, washed and dried
1 butter lettuce, washed and dried

Tropical Chicken Salad With
Raspberry Vinaigrette

1 small red onion,
   thinly sliced
1.5 kg chicken, roasted,
   skin removed and cut
   into bite-sized pieces
1 mango, peeled and
   sliced
1 pawpaw, peeled and
   sliced
1/3 cup halved pecans,
   toasted

DRESSING
1/2 cup olive oil
1/4 cup tinned
   raspberries with
   juice (see *Note*)
1 tablespoon white
   vinegar

1 teaspoon sesame oil
2 teaspoons honey
1/4 teaspoon Tabasco
   sauce
salt and pepper

1 Arrange all
ingredients for salad in
a serving bowl. Toss
well. Cover and
refrigerate until
required.
2 To prepare dressing,
place all ingredients in a
screw-top jar. Shake
well. Toss with salad
just before serving.

Note: Measure
raspberries and juice by
scooping fruit and juice
out of can together
using a measuring cup.
   If dressing is too
lumpy, place in a food
processor or blender.
Process until smooth.
   If fresh mango and
pawpaw are not
available, substitute
two 425 g cans of
mango and drain
well.
   Use a barbecued
chicken if desired.

Mosaic Terrine

Preparation time:
  30 minutes
Cooking time:
  1 hour
Serves 6
✻

2 thin baby carrots, quartered lengthways
1 small leek
2 small zucchini, quartered lengthways
6 asparagus spears
4 spring onions
8 spinach or young silverbeet leaves, blanched and refreshed
1 tablespoon fresh, chopped, mixed herbs
4 eggs
2 egg yolks
1½ cups milk
white pepper
spring onion greens, red lettuce leaves and steamed snow peas to decorate (optional)

1 Lightly cook carrots, leek, zucchini, asparagus and onions separately in water; drain and dry thoroughly on paper towels. Cut leek into quarters lengthways and discard most of its green top.
2 Place half the blanched spinach leaves in the base of a small buttered terrine or loaf tin. Arrange vegetables in terrine in layers, as desired, sprinkling each layer with some herbs.
3 Beat together eggs and egg yolks, milk and pepper. Pour slowly into terrine (some of the vegetables will float). Carefully place remaining spinach on top.
4 Cover terrine with foil, then with its lid. Place in a baking dish half-filled with water. Bake at 160°C for about 1 hour until set.
5 Remove lid and foil. Let stand in the oven with heat off, about 10 minutes more. Cool, but do not chill.
6 To serve, unmould and cut terrine into slices; arrange on serving plates. Decorate with thin spring onion strips, red lettuce and snow peas, if desired. Serve with a small dollop of Tomato-basil Coulis and Mustard Cream Sauce (see recipes).

Tomato-basil Coulis

Preparation time:
  15 minutes
Cooking time:
  nil
Serves 6
✻

500 g fresh ripe tomatoes, peeled and chopped
1 tablespoon chopped fresh basil (or ½ teaspoon dried)
2-3 teaspoons herb-flavoured wine vinegar
1 teaspoon sugar, or to taste
pepper

1 Press tomatoes through a fine sieve or mouli to remove seeds. Drain off any excess liquid.
2 Stir in basil, vinegar, sugar and pepper to taste. Chill until needed.

Mustard Cream Sauce

Preparation time:
  5 minutes
Cooking time:
  5 minutes
Serves 6
✻

1 tablespoon cornflour
1 tablespoon raw or caster sugar
2 teaspoons coarse-grained mustard
1/3 cup herb-flavoured wine vinegar
30 g unsalted butter
cayenne pepper
1 egg yolk, slightly beaten

*Mosaic Terrine served with Mustard Cream Sauce
(left) and Tomato-basil Coulis (right)*

½ cup thick cream

1 In a small saucepan, combine the cornflour, sugar, mustard, vinegar, butter and pepper. Cook, stirring constantly, over moderate heat until thickened and bubbly.

2 Remove from heat; beat in the egg yolk. Gradually stir in cream. Cover and cool until needed. Serve chilled.

19

Clockwise from top right:
Pineapple-mint Sorbet,
Raspberry Sorbet,
Blackcurrant Sorbet, Coconut
Sorbet, Champagne Sorbet
served with strawberries,
and Plum Sorbet served
with strawberries
and biscuits.

Festive Treats

Christmas cooking has its rewards. One of them is the sheer enjoyment your family can derive from delicious food, well-cooked and presented. Christmas is the one time of year most of us indulge a little without guilt, so it's fun to experiment with a variety of recipes. This chapter offers a wonderful collection of treats: new variations on traditional Christmas cakes and tarts, brandy snaps with a difference and mouthwatering desserts which make use of the fabulous selection of fruits available, from light sorbets to individual fruit tartlets.

CHRISTMAS SORBETS

Sorbets are so easy to make from sweetened, frozen fruit pulp or juice. Ideally, freeze the mixture in an ice-cream churn for a soft, snowy texture. Alternatively, still-freeze in shallow trays, break into manageable pieces and whip in a food processor until smooth, then return to the freezer. Both methods give excellent results.

Remove sorbets from freezer and allow to slightly soften before serving. Or, for convenience serving, scoop out balls and place on a foil-lined tray. Cover with freezer wrap; return to freezer.

Try mixing different colours and flavours in a pretty serving bowl.

Sorbet Syrup

**Preparation time:
2 minutes
Cooking time:
5-6 minutes
Makes about 6 cups syrup**
✳

**4 cups sugar
4 cups water**

1 Place sugar and water

in a saucepan. Stir over medium heat until sugar dissolves. Heat to boiling. Remove from heat and cool.

2 Refrigerate syrup in a covered jar or glass container until needed. Syrup keeps for up to 6 weeks.

STILL-FREEZE METHOD

Pour chilled sorbet mixture into shallow trays or baking tin. (Enamelled trays and tins or ones with an anodised coating are best to prevent changes in flavour, especially over long storage, and when acid liquids from lemons, grapefruit, passionfruit, tomato or wines are used.) Freeze until firm. Break into pieces; whip in a food processor until smooth. Return to trays; freeze.

Champagne Sorbet

Preparation time:
5 minutes plus churning or freezing
Cooking time:
nil
Serves 8
✳

Champagne sorbet is special, but this version

is even more special, since it is flavoured with raspberry eau-de-vie (available at larger bottle shops) and coloured with a little blackcurrant syrup.

750 mL bottle chilled champagne
1¼ cups Sorbet Syrup (see recipe)
¹/₃ cup raspberry eau-de-vie
¼ cup blackcurrant syrup

1 In a bowl, combine champagne, syrup, raspberry eau-de-vie and blackcurrant syrup. Chill, then freeze mixture in an ice-cream churn or still-freeze.

2 Serve as a between-courses refresher, or decorate with sliced fresh strawberries as a stunning dessert.

Raspberry Sorbet

Preparation time:
8 minutes plus churning or freezing
Cooking time:
nil
Makes 4 cups
✳

500 g raspberries, fresh or frozen
2 cups Sorbet Syrup (see recipe)
about ½ cup water

1 Heat together raspberries and syrup without boiling. Cool, then purée in a blender. Strain the seeds through a sieve.

2 Measure purée, add enough water to make 4 cups total. Chill mixture, freeze in ice-cream churn or still-freeze.

Blackcurrant Sorbet

Preparation time:
8 minutes plus churning or freezing
Cooking time:
nil
Serves 8
✳

500 g blackcurrants, fresh or frozen
3½ cups Sorbet Syrup (see recipe)

1 Heat together blackcurrants and syrup without boiling. Cool, then purée in a blender. Push mixture through a

23

nylon sieve or strain through muslin; discard seeds and other hard bits.
2 Chill, then freeze in an ice-cream churn or still-freeze.

Coconut Sorbet

Preparation time:
   12 minutes plus churning or freezing
Cooking time:
   nil
Serves 8
✳

1 teaspoon plain
   gelatine
1¾ cups cold water
¾ cup sugar
400 mL canned
   coconut milk
chocolate or toasted
   coconut to decorate
   (optional)

1 Sprinkle gelatine over ¼ cup water; leave to let gelatine soften.
2 Combine sugar and remaining 1½ cups water in a pan; stir over medium heat to dissolve sugar. Heat to boiling; remove from heat and stir in gelatine until dissolved. Stir in coconut milk.
3 Chill, then freeze in ice-cream churn or still-

freeze. Serve decorated with chocolate curls or shapes prepared from melted, poured and cooled chocolate if desired, or add some toasted and shredded coconut.

Pineapple-mint Sorbet

Preparation time:
   10 minutes plus chilling and churning or freezing
Cooking time:
   nil
Serves 8
✳

1 ripe pineapple,
   peeled
1½ cups Sorbet Syrup
   (see recipe)
½ cup fresh mint
   leaves, finely
   chopped
mint sprigs to decorate
   (optional)

1 Cut pineapple lengthways into quarters; remove the hard woody core. Purée in pieces in a blender, then strain through a nylon sieve, pushing through as much juice and pulp as possible. Discard all the fibres (you should have 2½ cups of pulp).
2 Combine pulp with syrup and mint. Chill,

then freeze in an ice-cream churn or still-freeze.
3 Serve garnished with mint sprigs, if desired.

Plum Sorbet

Preparation time:
   15 minutes plus churning or freezing
Cooking time:
   nil
Serves 8
✳

2 cups fresh plum
   purée (see *Note*)
3 cups Sorbet Syrup
   (see recipe)
½ cup orange juice
¼ cup lemon juice

1 For purée, pour boiling water over whole plums in a bowl, leave 1 minute, then plunge into cold water. Remove skins; cut flesh from seeds. Purée pulp in a blender or food processor to yield 2 cups purée.
2 In a bowl, mix together pulp, syrup, orange and lemon juices. Chill, freeze mixture in an ice-cream churn or still-freeze.

Note: Plums vary in size — and pulp content — by type, so use your judgement on quantity required for 2 cups purée.

Festive Fruit Salad served with a traditional Christmas pudding

Festive Fruit Salad

Preparation time:
  17 minutes
Cooking time:
  nil
Serves 10
✱

1 × 250 g punnet
  strawberries, washed
  and hulled
½ rockmelon, balled or
  cut into chunks
2 kiwi fruit, peeled and
  sliced
2 oranges, segmented
2 apples, chopped
2 bananas, sliced
  thickly

½ cup sugar
300 mL water
¼ cup Cointreau

MANGO MASCARPONE
250 g mascarpone
  cheese
425 g canned mango
  slices, drained

1 Combine all fruit in a
large bowl (see *Note*).
Bring sugar and water
to the boil in a small
pan, stirring constantly.
Do not stir once boiled.
2 Simmer syrup for 1
minute, then cool. Stir
in Cointreau. Pour over
fruit, mixing well.
Refrigerate, stirring

occasionally.
3 To prepare mango
mascarpone, place
cheese and mango in a
food processor or
blender. Process until
smooth. Serve with fruit
salad.

Note: Slice apples and
bananas and brush
with lemon juice just
before mixing with
syrup, to prevent
browning. Any
combination of canned
or fresh fruit may be
used, such as other
melons, grapes, mango,
stone fruits, etc.

25

Brandy Snap Baskets with Mascarpone and Fruit

Preparation time:
 30 minutes
Cooking time:
 5 minutes
Makes 12
✳✳

**BRANDY SNAP
 BASKETS**
60 g butter
¼ cup brown sugar
¼ cup golden syrup
¼ cup plain flour
**½ teaspoon ground
 ginger**
1 teaspoon lemon juice
**¼ teaspoon imitation
 vanilla essence**

FILLING
**1 tablespoon rum
 (see *Note*)**
**200 g mascarpone
 cheese (see *Note*)**
**fruit of choice, e.g.
 peaches, apricots,
 nectarines,
 strawberries (see
 Note)**

*Brandy Snap Baskets With
Mascarpone And Fruit*

1 To make brandy snap baskets, place butter, sugar and syrup in a small pan. Heat gently until butter melts and sugar dissolves. Cool.
2 Sift flour and ginger together. Stir into butter mixture with lemon juice and vanilla.

3 Place teaspoonfuls of mixture onto a greased tray (about 4 per tray). Allow room for spreading.
4 Bake at 180°C for about 5 minutes or until golden. Allow to cool on tray for 1 minute.
5 Remove from tray with a spatula. Place each brandy snap over an upturned glass. Shape into a basket with fingers. Cool completely. Continue with remaining mixture.
6 To make filling: stir rum into mascarpone. Spoon into baskets. Top

with fruit just before serving.

Note: ● Other liqueurs may be used to flavour mascarpone, such as Cointreau or Grand Marnier.
● Mascarpone is an Italian-style cream cheese available from delicatessens.
● Prepare fresh fruit by stoning and slicing or chopping into pieces.
● Drained canned fruit such as passionfruit, mango, peaches and apricots may be substituted when fresh fruits are not available.

26

Bûche de Noel

Preparation time:
   50 minutes
Cooking time:
   15-20 minutes
Serves 10
✳✳✳

CAKE
3 eggs
¾ cup caster sugar
1 cup self-raising flour
¼ cup cocoa
⅓ cup water
extra caster sugar

FILLING
300 mL thickened
   cream
2 tablespoons icing
   sugar
1 tablespoon cocoa

ICING
60 g butter
60 g cooking chocolate
2 cups icing sugar,
   sifted
1 teaspoon imitation
   vanilla essence
2 tablespoons milk

CHOCOLATE CURLS
180 g cooking
   chocolate
icing sugar

1 To prepare cake, place eggs in the small bowl of an electric mixer. Beat until thick and creamy. Add sugar gradually, beating until thick and sugar has dissolved.
2 Sift flour and cocoa together at least twice to ensure they are well combined. Fold into egg mixture, followed by water.
3 Pour mixture into a greased, greaseproof-paper-lined Swiss roll tin. Spread out evenly. Bake at 180° C for 15–20 minutes or until cake springs back when touched.
4 Sprinkle a tea towel with extra caster sugar. Turn cake onto this. Peel off paper. Trim off crusts. Roll up from long side, taking tea towel with the cake. Cool.
5 To prepare filling, whip cream with icing sugar and cocoa until stiff peaks form. Cover and refrigerate.
6 To prepare icing, melt butter and chocolate together in a small pan over low heat. Cool slightly. Beat in remaining ingredients. Add more milk if necessary to produce a spreadable consistency. Keep at room

Bûche de Noel

27

temperature.

7 To prepare chocolate curls, melt chocolate over low heat. Spread onto a marble slab or other smooth surface to about 1 cm thick. Cool

until just set. Scrape a knife held horizontally to chocolate over surface, to produce curls. Set aside in a cool place.

8 To assemble log, unroll cake. Spread with filling. Re-roll. Cut a diagonal slice from one end of the cake to make the 'knot'. Cover cake with icing. Press 'knot' onto top of cake. Cover with icing.

9 Make a spiral pattern in the 'knot' and at both ends of the cake to resemble wood. Arrange curls over cake, pressing in lightly if necessary. Dust top and base of cake with icing sugar to resemble snow. Refrigerate until required. Slice to serve.

Continental Almond Torte

Preparation time:
  20 minutes
Cooking time:
  35 minutes
Makes 1 cake
✳✳

250 g butter, softened
1 cup caster sugar
½ teaspoon almond
  essence

4 eggs
1 cup self-raising flour
½ cup cornflour
pinch of salt
½ cup finely ground
  almonds

FILLING
600 mL cream
2 tablespoons icing
  sugar
1 cup sliced
  strawberries
about 1 tablespoon
  orange liqueur

Continental Almond Torte

½ cup toasted flaked
almonds
about 1 tablespoon
almond liqueur
extra whole
strawberries and
toasted almonds to
garnish
extra icing sugar to
garnish

1 Beat together butter,
sugar and essence until
light and creamy. Beat
in eggs, one at a time,
until blended.
2 Sift together flour,
cornflour and salt;
gradually stir into egg
mixture. Stir in ground
almonds.
3 Turn batter into two
greased and paper-lined
20 cm round cake tins.
Bake for 30–35 minutes
at 180°C until cake
springs back when
touched. Turn out and
cool completely on a
wire rack.
4 To make filling, beat
cream and icing sugar
until stiff. Divide in
half. Stir in sliced
strawberries and 1
tablespoon orange
liqueur into one
portion; flaked almonds
and 1 tablespoon
almond liqueur into the
other.
5 Split cake layers in
half horizontally.
Drizzle each layer with
extra liqueur to taste.
Spread each filling over

Individual Fruit Tartlets

two of the four layers,
then stack layers
alternately on serving
platter. Garnish with
strawberries and
almonds; sprinkle with
sifted icing sugar. Chill
until served.

Individual Fruit Tartlets

Preparation time:
20 minutes
Cooking time:
6 minutes
Makes 10

✳✳

½ quantity sweet
shortcrust pastry (see
recipe for *Fruit
Mince Pies* on
page 33)

FILLING
2 eggs
4 egg yolks
½ cup caster sugar
2 cups milk
2 tablespoons plain
flour
2 tablespoons
cornflour
fresh and canned fruit
of choice
½ cup apricot conserve

1 Prepare pastry
following instructions
for Fruit Mince Pies.
2 Ease into 10 tartlet
tins. Line each tartlet
with a piece of
greaseproof paper and
sprinkle with dried
beans or rice. Bake at
220°C for 10 minutes,
then remove the beans
and paper and bake for
a further 10 minutes or
until golden and cooked

through. Cool on a wire rack.

3 To make filling, whisk together eggs, egg yolks and sugar. Mix a little of the milk with combined flours to form a smooth paste. Whisk into egg mixture.

4 Heat remaining milk in a small pan until almost boiling. Remove from heat and whisk into egg mixture. Pour this mixture back into pan. Heat, stirring constantly, until mixture boils and thickens. Simmer for 3 minutes. Cool slightly. Spread over base of prepared tartlets.

5 Arrange fruit decoratively on top of custard. Melt apricot conserve over low heat and brush over fruit to glaze. Remove tartlets from tins just before serving.

Light and Golden Fruit Cake

Preparation time:
15 minutes
Cooking time:
1¾-2 hours
Makes 1 cake
✳

1⅓ cups glacé cherries, halved
⅔ cup golden sultanas

Light and Golden Fruit Cake

½ cup each chopped glacé apricots and pineapple
⅓ cup chopped mixed peel
½ cup blanched almonds, coarsely chopped
2 cups plain flour
1 teaspoon baking powder
¼ teaspoon salt
250 g butter, softened
1 tablespoon each grated orange and lemon rind
1 cup caster sugar
5 eggs
¼ cup sweet sherry

1 Combine fruits and almonds and then toss with ¼ cup of flour. Sift together the remaining flour, baking powder and salt.

2 Beat butter with grated rind, gradually adding sugar, until thick and creamy. Beat in eggs, one at a time. Stir in flour alternately with sherry. Fold in the fruit-nut mixture.

3 Turn into a greased, lined, deep 20 cm square tin. Bake at 160°C for 1¾-2 hours until firm, cool slightly, turn out and cool completely. Wrap airtight and store.

Chocolate Profiteroles

Preparation time:
25 minutes
Cooking time:
25 minutes
Makes 12
✳✳✳

CHOUX PASTRY
2 tablespoons butter
150 mL water
½ cup plus 2 tablespoons self-raising wholemeal flour, sifted
1 egg
1 egg white

CHOCOLATE SAUCE
⅓ cup chopped dark cooking chocolate
⅓ cup water
1 teaspoon arrowroot

300 mL thickened reduced cream, whipped
icing sugar for dusting

1 To make pastry, heat butter and water in pan over moderately-low heat until boiling. Reduce heat. Add sifted flour all at once; beat vigorously with wooden spoon until dough makes a ball that cleans the side of the pan.
2 Remove from heat and cool slightly. Beat together egg and egg white; gradually add to dough, beating well until smooth and glossy.

3 Spoon heaped teaspoonfuls of dough into 12 mounds on a lightly floured baking tray (or use a piping bag). Bake at 200°C for 20 minutes until puffed, firm and golden. Cut a tiny slit in each puff to release steam; cool completely on wire rack (see *Note*).
4 To make sauce, in small pan over low heat, melt chocolate with all but 2 tablespoons of water, stirring until smooth. Blend arrowroot with reserved water; stir into chocolate.
5 Cook, stirring until thickened and bubbly.

Transfer to a bowl. Cover surface directly with clear plastic wrap. Cool completely.
6 To serve, pipe whipped cream into puffs to fill. Pile onto a serving plate. Lightly sprinkle with icing sugar (if using). Drizzle sauce over. Serve.

Note: If desired, puffs can be prepared to this point and stored airtight at room temperature overnight. Or, freeze up to four months in a rigid container. Reheat at 180°C to thaw and refresh; cool before filling.

Chocolate Profiteroles

Frozen Fruit Pudding

Preparation time:
5 minutes plus overnight standing and freezing
Cooking time:
nil
Serves 8–10
✳

1 cup raisins, chopped
½ cup sultanas
½ cup currants
1 × 100 g packet red glacé cherries, halved
¼ cup chopped dried apricots
juice and finely grated rind of 1 orange
¼ cup brandy
½ cup cream
2 litres chocolate ice-cream, softened
½ cup extra cream
1 tablespoon Tia Maria or Kahlua
1 litre vanilla ice-cream, softened
whipped cream and maraschino cherries, to serve

1 Combine fruit and brandy in a bowl. Stand overnight or longer if possible.
2 Fold cream and fruit into chocolate ice-cream. Pour into a 12-cup ice-cream mould. Freeze until firm.
3 Fold extra cream and liqueur into vanilla ice-cream. Pour over chocolate mixture. Re-freeze ice-cream until needed.
4 To un-mould pudding: dip base into hot water for a few seconds. Wipe sides of mould with a cloth which has been dipped in hot water. Invert onto a plate. Serve with whipped cream and maraschino cherries.

Steamed Christmas Pudding

Preparation time:
30 minutes
Cooking time:
5–6 hours
Serves 8–10
✳

2 cups sultanas
1½ cups raisins
¾ cup currants
1 tablespoon finely chopped mixed peel
¼ cup brandy
¼ cup rum
250 g butter
1 cup brown sugar
5 eggs
1 cup plain flour
½ teaspoon bicarbonate of soda
1½ teaspoons mixed spice
125 g fresh breadcrumbs
¼ cup chopped almonds

1 Combine fruits, peel, brandy and rum in a bowl. Cream butter and sugar together. Add eggs, one at a time, beating well after each addition. Gradually add flour, bicarbonate of soda and spice. Fold in fruit mixture, breadcrumbs and chopped almonds.
2 Spoon into a well-greased 8-cup pudding

Clockwise from back: Frozen Fruit Pudding, Steamed Christmas Pudding, Brandy Butter and Brandy Cream

Brandy Cream

Preparation time:
 8 minutes
Cooking time:
 nil
Makes about 4 cups
✳

¼ cup brandy
300 mL cream,
 whipped
2 eggs, separated
½ cup caster sugar

1 Fold brandy into cream. Beat egg whites until soft peaks form. Gradually add sugar. Beat till thick, glossy and sugar has dissolved.
2 Beat in egg yolks. Fold in cream mixture. Store in refrigerator.

Brandy Butter

Preparation time:
 5 minutes
Cooking time:
 nil
Makes about 1 cup
✳

250 g butter
⅓ cup firmly packed
 brown sugar
1 cup icing sugar, sifted
¼ cup brandy

1 Cream butter and sugars together until the mixture is smooth.
2 Add brandy gradually, beating continuously. Chill in the refrigerator until required.

basin. Allow room for pudding to rise. Cover (see *Note*). Place in a large saucepan. Fill pan with hot water, two-thirds up the sides of the pudding basin. Bring to the boil and boil rapidly for 5–6 hours. Check water level occasionally and refill as needed. Cool the pudding completely. Then store it in

refrigerator.
3 To serve: reheat pudding by cooking in the same way for 1 hour before needed. Serve with hot Brandy Cream or Butter (see recipes).

Note: Cover with greased greaseproof paper then foil. Tie with string, leaving a loop for a handle for easier lifting.

Gourmet Gifts

Clockwise from top right: Almond-walnut Puffs, Spiced Hazelnuts and Apricot Brandy Balls, Date Delights with Marzipan Liqueur Loaf and Ginger-nut Chocolates, and on the platter at left, Fruit Nut Wreaths with Chocolate Orange Truffles and Apricot Splits

Flavoured Oil

Preparation time:
  **10 minutes plus
  5 days standing**
Cooking time:
  nil
Makes 2 cups
✱

**2 cups vegetable oil
2-3 tablespoons
  chopped fresh herbs
  of choice, or 2-3
  cloves crushed garlic,
  or 2-3 chopped
  chillies, or ¼ cup
  chopped walnuts
fresh whole pieces of
  chosen flavouring**

1 Heat oil in a double
saucepan. Add
flavouring. Remove
from heat. Cover and
leave to stand for 5
days.
2 Strain into a sterilised
bottle. Add fresh, whole
pieces of flavouring to
the bottle.

3 Cork and label. Store
in a cool place.

Flavoured Vinegar

Preparation time:
  **10 minutes plus 5
  days standing**
Cooking time:
  nil
Makes 2 cups
✱

**2 cups white vinegar
2-3 tablespoons
  chopped fresh herbs
  of choice,
dried apricots and
  raspberries; or
1 onion, chopped; or
2-3 cloves crushed
  garlic; or
1 tablespoon cracked
  peppercorns (see
  Note)
fresh whole pieces of
  chosen flavouring**

1 Heat vinegar in a

small pan until
simmering. Remove
from heat. Add
flavouring.
2 Cover and allow to
stand for 5 days, stirring
occasionally.
3 Strain into a sterilised
bottle. Add fresh pieces
of flavouring to bottle.

*Left to right: Delhi
Chutney and a selection
of flavoured oils and
vinegars*

HINTS

- Sterilise jars by placing in a large saucepan. Cover
with cold water. Bring to the boil. Simmer for 5
minutes. Remove bottles. Invert on paper towels. Allow
to dry thoroughly in a warm oven.
- Once any of the sealed jars are opened, store in the
refrigerator.
- Collect bottles and jars through the year as many
products you purchase come in lovely containers. This
is not only a good exercise in recycling it is also a
good money-saving idea.
- Make your food gifts as far ahead as possible to
avoid a last-minute rush. If posting, use a box and lots
of wadding.

4 onions, chopped

2 green apples, peeled, cored and chopped

1 cup chopped dates (see *Note*)

2 teaspoons dry mustard

1 teaspoon curry powder

½ teaspoon cayenne pepper

½ teaspoon ground ginger

4 cups white vinegar (see *Note*)

2 cups brown sugar

1 Place all the ingredients except sugar in a large pan. Bring to the boil. Simmer, uncovered, for about 1 hour or until thick, stirring occasionally.

2 Add sugar. Stir chutney over gentle heat until sugar dissolves.

3 Bring to the boil. Boil, uncovered, for 5–10 minutes. Pour into hot sterilised jars. Seal, label and store in a cool place for up to 12 months.

Note: ● Chop dates easily by snipping with scissors.

● Add extra vinegar if chutney is becoming very thick.

4 Cork tightly. Label and store in a cool place. Keeps well for several months.

Note: Peppercorns only need to be cracked to allow the flavour to be released into the vinegar.

Delhi Chutney

Preparation time:
20 minutes
Cooking time:
1¼ hours
Makes 4-5 cups
*

425 g canned mangoes, drained

Whisky Nut Balls

Preparation time:
  **30 minutes plus
  overnight standing**
Cooking time:
  5 minutes
Makes 25
✳

about 25 pecan halves
¼-½ cup whisky
500 g icing sugar
60 g butter, softened
100 g cooking
  chocolate, in pieces
½ tablespoon white
  vegetable shortening

1 Soak pecans in
enough whisky to cover
completely in a covered
jar overnight. Drain,
reserving the whisky
marinade.
2 Beat half the icing
sugar with butter until
creamy. In a separate
bowl, combine
remaining icing sugar
and reserved whisky;
gradually stir into
creamed mixture. Chill
until firm enough to
shape.
3 With fingers, shape
mixture around each
pecan, rolling into small
ovals. Chill until firm.
4 Melt chocolate and
shortening in a bowl
over hot water, stirring
until smooth. Arrange
ovals on wire rack over
greaseproof paper to
catch drippings.

Spoon teaspoonsful of
chocolate over ovals
to coat.
5 Let stand until
hardened in a cool place
or the refrigerator.
Store in a cool, dry place
in an airtight container.
The longer they stand,
the more mellow the
flavour.

Merry Pudding Morsels

Preparation time:
  30 minutes
Cooking time:
  nil
Makes about 36
✳

500 g dense, moist fruit
  cake or boiled
  pudding
little brandy or orange
  juice
Royal Icing (see
  recipe page 46)
red and green glacé
  cherries, chopped

1 Using a melon-baller,
scoop out balls of cake.
Roll balls between
hands if necessary to
make them smooth. Use
a little juice if necessary
to moisten cake.
2 Brush lightly with

brandy to flavour, if
desired. Let stand a few
minutes to dry.
3 Prepare Royal Icing as
directed. Pipe or spoon
icing over tops of balls,
allowing it to drizzle
slightly down sides.
Sprinkle with cherries.
Stand until hardened.
4 Store in a single layer
in airtight containers or
wrap individually,
resting on tiny
cardboard squares in
clear cellophane paper.

Tiny Fruit Cakes

Preparation time:
  **30 minutes plus
  overnight standing**
Cooking time:
  30-40 minutes
Makes 24
✳

1 cup mixed dried fruit
1 cup golden sultanas
½ cup brandy
125 g butter
¼ cup packed brown
  sugar
1 tablespoon grated
  orange rind
¼ cup orange
  marmalade
2 eggs
1 cup plain flour
2 teaspoons mixed
  spice
1 cup walnut pieces
  (optional, see *Note*)
glacé cherries and
  sliced almonds to
  decorate

Clockwise from left: Tiny Fruit Cakes,
Sweetmeats, Whisky Nut Balls and Merry Pudding Morsels.

1 Combine fruits and ¼ cup of brandy. Cover and marinate overnight.
2 Cream butter, sugar and orange peel until light; add marmalade and eggs and beat until fluffy.
3 Sift together flour and spice. Toss in walnuts (see *Note*) and

marinated fruit to coat well. Add to creamed mixture and mix well.
4 Spoon into lightly greased foil-lined paper patty cases in standard muffin tins, filling half full. Top with cherries and almonds.
5 Bake at 160°C for 30–40 minutes until a

toothpick inserted in the centre comes out clean. Do not overbake. (A pan of water on the bottom oven shelf will keep cakes moist while baking.)
6 Cool completely, then spoon remaining brandy over each. Wrap in plastic film. Store at

Remove cinnamon sticks.

3 Place prunes in sterilised jars. Pour over syrup to completely cover. Seal and label. Store in a cool place. Leave for about a week before using. When properly stored, prunes will keep for up to 12 months.

Sherried Raisins

Preparation time:
  10 minutes
Cooking time:
  nil
Makes about 2 cups
✻

375 g raisins
2 tablespoons slivered almonds
1 ring glacé pineapple, cut into thin strips
1 cup dry sherry (see *Note*)

1 Place raisins, almonds and glacé pineapple in alternate layers in sterilised jars. Add enough sherry to completely cover.
2 Seal and label. Store in a cool place. Raisins will keep well for up to 12 months.

Note: More sherry than 1 cup may be required. Use enough to cover raisins.

Truffles

Preparation time:
  30 minutes plus chilling
Cooking time:
  nil
Makes about 40
✻

90 g butter
½ cup thickened cream
300 g dark chocolate pieces
2 tablespoons brandy (see *Note*)
cocoa

1 Place butter and cream in a small pan. Heat until butter melts, and mixture boils.
2 Add chocolate. Stir over low heat until melted. Cool, then stir in brandy. Transfer mixture to a bowl.
3 Cool in the refrigerator, stirring occasionally. When firm enough to handle, form teaspoonsful of mixture into uneven balls.
4 Sift some cocoa onto greaseproof paper. Roll

each truffle in the cocoa until they are all generously coated. Refrigerate until firm. Store in an airtight container.
5 Truffles keep for about 2 weeks in the refrigerator and about 6 weeks if frozen.

Note: Whisky and some other spirit or liqueur may be used in place of brandy.

VARIATION
White Truffles: as for Truffles but replace dark chocolate with white chocolate. The brandy can be replaced with Tia Maria. Coat White Truffles in coconut instead of cocoa.

Christmas Shortbread

Preparation time:
  15 minutes
Cooking time:
  30-35 minutes
Makes 16 wedges
✻

2 cups plain flour
2 tablespoons rice flour or ground rice (see *Note*)
250 g butter, cut into cubes

Christmas Shortbread

⅓ cup caster sugar

1 Sift dry ingredients together into a bowl. Add butter. Rub in using fingertips. Press mixture together.
2 Turn out onto a lightly floured surface. Knead gently. Divide into two. Mould into rounds about 1 cm thick on greased baking trays.
3 Decorate edges. Mark out eight equal portions on each round. Prick with a fork. Bake at 160°C for 30–35 minutes.
4 Allow shortbread to stand for 10 minutes. Cool on a wire rack. Store Shortbread for up to 2 weeks in an airtight container.
5 Alternatively, press mixture into shortbread moulds which have been well dusted with cornflour. Flatten base. Tap out onto greased baking trays. Bake as directed.

Note: Rice flour and ground rice are sold at health food shops.
Shortbread moulds are available at most specialty kitchen shops and also at major department stores.

Nature's Bounty

Fresh and Green

Christmas Crafts

Glittering Garland

*C*hristmas is one of those times when the budget may find itself stretched to the limit. Here's where home-made gifts come to the rescue.

You can give Grandma a luxurious satin coathanger, make your aunt a Christmas wreath, give your nieces and nephews a useful box beautifully covered (by your children of course) with coloured paper, stars, spangles and anything else they can think of, and make delightful Christmas decorations you can hang on the tree.

WELCOME WREATHS

No special skills are required to make these wreaths (only one relies on needle and thread), just check our preparation advice to make sure you've time to finish your favourite.

Nature's Bounty

twig wreath base
string
medium florist's stem wires
selection of dried flowers, seed pods, e.g. honesty, pine cones, wheat sheaves, and red berries

1 Attach a string loop to wreath base for hanging. Trim stems of dried flowers and pods to about 6 cm and strengthen by winding wire around each. Wire each cone around base.
2 Attach larger flowers first, with brightest colours at the centre to add depth. Tuck in seed pods, pine cones and wheat. Place honesty and other light-coloured pieces around the edge.
3 Fill any gaps with small clusters of flowers and position tiny bright berries last so they don't get hidden. Aim for a good balance of colour and an even shape.

Glittering Garland

wire coathanger
50 cm of 90 cm-wide thick polyester wadding
needle and thread
8 m silver tinsel
4 m each gold and blue cord
3 m wide gold ribbon
20 cm blue tulle
silver and gold apple baubles

1 Bend coathanger to form a ring. Cut wadding in half lengthways and wrap around the ring, stitching to hold.

2 Wind tinsel around ring to cover wadding. Cut 20 cm from ribbon and position the remaining ribbon around the outside of the wreath. Bind in place with blue and gold cord, knotting ends at top. Tie baubles to cord at top.

3 Fold ends of tulle to centre to form a bow. Fix in place by tying long ends of main ribbon into a bow over it, leaving long ribbon tails. Tuck the 20 cm strip of ribbon into the knot to make short false tails.

Christmas Bonbons

Fresh and Green

wire coathanger
florist's stem wires
green foliage e.g. off-
   cuts from Christmas
   tree, pine, cypress,
   ivy, holly
string of gilt beads
flowers, fresh or fabric
2 m narrow green
   ribbon
2 m wide red ribbon

1 Bend hanger to form a ring. Using stem wires, attach larger pieces of foliage to the ring then add smaller pieces.

2 Wind string of beads around wreath, then tuck in the flowers. Cut green ribbon into 50 cm lengths. Slip each length through string of beads and tie in a bow. Use red ribbon to tie a large bow at the top of the wreath.

Note: To keep foliage fresh, plunge into a bucket of water immediately after cutting and leave to soak until required. For a longer-lasting wreath, wrap soaked moss around ring, using old pantihose to secure.

Regularly spray wreath with water.

Note: Wire wreaths can be purchased from florists or garden centres and are easier to work with.

Christmas Bonbons

Handmade bonbons will add a touch of flair to your Christmas festivities. They're easy to make — and easy on the budget.

cardboard cylinders
   from toilet rolls
white bond paper
tissue paper
crêpe paper or
   wrapping paper for
   outer cover
curling ribbon or
   ribbon oddments
old Christmas cards,
   wrapping paper or
   cardboard for motifs
friction strips
   (optional; available
   from distributors of
   paper products and
   party novelties)
paper doilies for lacy
   bonbons
scissors
pinking shears
glue stick
fillers e.g. party hats,
   sweets, small gifts,
   jokes or riddles,
   balloons

1 For each bonbon, cut
white bond paper 21 ×
15 cm (half A4 sheet),
tissue paper 25 × 17 cm
and paper for outer
cover 29 x 19 cm, using
pinking shears if
desired.

2 Place the cylinder on
the centre of the paper

as shown in picture. If
desired, place a friction
strip between the
cylinder and the bond
paper. Place a spare
cylinder at each end of
the centre cylinder to
hold the ends of the
cracker in shape. Roll
papers firmly around
the cylinders and glue in
place along the long
edge.

3 Ease one of the spare
cylinders out about 2
cm, away from the
centre cylinder and tie a
ribbon between the
cylinders, gathering up
the papers. Remove the
spare cylinder and pull
end tight with the
ribbon, finishing with a
secure knot.
4 Drop in the gift, hat,
joke etc and tie the
remaining end the same
way as the first end.
5 Cut the ends into
peaks or if you have cut
the paper with pinking
shears, leave ends long.
For a lacy bonbon, glue
strips cut from paper
doilies to the right side

of the outer paper ends
before rolling.

6 Add motifs cut out
from old Christmas
cards, wrapping paper
or cardboard and glue
directly onto bonbon.
Or glue motif onto a
strip cut out from
contrasting paper, then
glue the strip around
the bonbon. For a
personal touch, write
names on the labels.

TO MAKE
PAPER HATS
Cut a strip of crepe
paper approx 62 cm
long x 5 cm wide.
Overlap the ends about
1.5 cm (or to fit around
head) and glue ends
together. Cut one edge
to form peaks as in a
crown.

Beautiful Stylish Boxes

Stylish Boxes

coloured tissue paper
gift wrap
boxes
variety of ribbon
   and cord ties
stars and other
   trims
scissors
glue
tape

Presenting your Christmas gifts in boxes makes them seem special. You can decorate your own easily and inexpensively. Save boxes during the year, and cover them with foil or bright gift wrap. Finish with generous ribbon bows. For economical wrapping, choose sheets of red and green tissue paper or even plain white paper, then use your imagination to decorate them. Tie with strips of contrasting tissue. Be generous with stick-on stars, trims, rick-rack braid, silver cord and other ties.

CHRISTMAS DECORATIONS

With delightful Christmas decorations like these hanging on your tree, you need never be short of a last-minute gift.

They're pretty and practical, and so easy and inexpensive to make. Fill them with sweet-smelling lavender or potpourri, and they'll scent any drawer or bedside table long after the festive season is over.

Christmas Mice

These cute little mice are easily made using a minimum of materials and will be sure to delight your family and friends.

white felt (1 square will make 5 mice)
red felt (1 square will make 8 shawls)
Christmas print fabric for dress
print fabric for bonnet
silver gift cord
small black glass beads for eyes
50 cm of 1 cm-wide lace
40 cm of 1 cm-wide green ribbon
glue
black thread

Soap and Lavender Bonbon, Christmas Mouse and Soap Bag

wadding
potpourri or lavender (optional)

1 MOUSE. Trace mouse pattern (actual size) onto paper. Cut out two mouse pieces from white felt. Place felt together and sew a seam less than 5 mm around outside edge of mouse, leaving bottom edge open for stuffing.
2 Fill with wadding (or use lavender or potpourri), pushing tightly up into nose and

head area to form shape. Fill body, and sew seam closed along bottom edge. Trim excess felt around seams to neaten.
3 DRESS. Cut a 12 × 20 cm rectangle from Christmas print fabric. Turn one 20 cm edge under twice for hem and other 20 cm edge under once for neck. Attach lace to skirt and stitch hems. (Hem and lace together form a stand for mouse.) With right sides facing, stitch

Lavender Umbrella,
Christmas Fairy and
Christmas Stocking

thread doubled, tie a knot on the end leaving a 2 cm tail to form whiskers. Place threaded needle into the right cheek and bring out through the left upper side of the mouse's face at position of eye. Thread a black glass bead for the eye onto the needle, then stitch close to the same spot to secure eye. Bring needle back through the nose area. Finish the nose with a few stitches. Repeat for second eye and whiskers.

Lavender Sachet

Christmas print fabric
80 cm of 2 cm-wide
**   lace**
1 m of 1 cm-wide
**   ribbon**
lavender

1 From print fabric, cut a 24 cm-diameter circle. Fold in half, press and cut in two. Sew lace to right side of outer edge of each piece. Fold semi-circle, with right sides together, into a cone shape and sew seam. Turn right side out and half-fill with lavender.
2 Gather up material tightly around lavender by hand-stitching or secure using a rubber

back seam. Gather up neckline with small running stitches and sew to back of mouse's neck to secure.
4 BONNET. Cut an 8 cm-diameter circle from small print fabric. Sew lace around edge, overlapping ends. Gather up bonnet just inside lace edge and fill bonnet with a little wadding. Secure to mouse's head with little stitches at front and back. Cut a 2 cm square of white felt. Cut

crossways to form two triangles. Fold each triangle over to form ears and glue to side of bonnet.
5 SHAWL. From a 12 cm square of red felt, cut two triangles (makes 2 shawls). Wrap around mouse, overlapping at front; secure with a few tiny stitches. Add a small bow to overlap. Attach cord loop to back neck of mouse for easy tying to tree.
6 FACE. Using black

57

band. To make a ribbon hanger, double the ribbon and tie a knot 8 cm from the doubled end to form a hanger. Secure inside gathered section of sachet and cover with a ribbon bow.

Note: These materials make 2 sachets.

Soap Bags

**Christmas print fabric
30 cm of 3 cm-wide
   lace
oval shaped soap**

**40 cm of 1 cm-wide
   ribbon**

1 Cut a 13 × 22 cm rectangle of fabric. Turn under one long edge twice and press hem. Sew lace along the right side of this edge.
2 With right sides together, join to make centre back seam. Sew another seam across base; turn to right side. Wrap soap in a paper tissue to prevent soap from chipping or rubbing through fabric.

Place in bag and secure with a small rubber band. Trim with a ribbon bow.

Soap and Lavender Bonbons

**Christmas print fabric
30 cm of 3-4 cm-wide
   lace
oval shaped soap,
   lavender or
   potpourri
rubber bands**

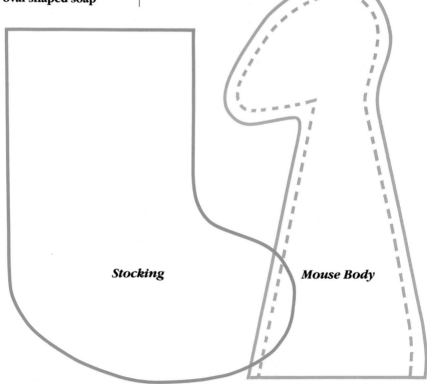

Stocking

Mouse Body

70 cm of 1 cm-wide ribbon

1 Cut a 15 × 20 cm rectangle from fabric. Turn short sides under twice and press hems. Sew lace on right side of fabric along these short sides. With right sides together, sew a centre back seam.
2 Turn tube shape right side out and secure one end where lace meets fabric with a rubber band. Insert soap, lavender or potpourri and secure other end with another small rubber band. Trim each band with a ribbon bow.

Christmas Fairy

soft white net fabric
small plastic doll
large red silk flower for skirts
small white or red silk flower for hat
50 cm of 1 cm-wide ribbon
lavender or potpourri
glue
rubber bands

1 Cut net material into a 20 cm-diameter circle. Place two tablespoons of lavender or potpourri in the centre of the net.
2 Take apart the large red silk flower (this can make three or four

skirts). Make a small slit in the centre of one skirt and push doll's legs through. Gather up net material with lavender in your hand and push doll's legs down into the middle of the lavender. Secure with a rubber band. Glue on a small silk flower for a hat.
3 To make a ribbon hanger, double the ribbon and tie a knot 8 cm from the doubled end to form a hanger. Place around the doll's waist with the hanger at the back and finish with a bow in front.

Christmas Stocking

red felt rectangle 10 × 18 cm
10 cm of 5 cm-wide lace
wadding
pattern paper

1 Cut out stocking pattern (actual size) on paper. Fold felt in half and cut out two stocking pieces. Sew lace across top of each piece.
2 With right sides facing, using a 3 mm seam allowance, sew around edge of stocking leaving top open for stuffing. Turn right side

out. Fill with wadding. Using double thread, make a loop at stocking back for hanging.

Lavender Umbrella

Christmas print fabric
80 cm of 2 cm-wide lace
80 cm of 1 cm-wide ribbon
30 cm chenille stick (pipe-cleaner)
lavender

1 Follow Lavender Sachet directions, but leave a small opening at the base of the cone shape.
2 With right sides of fabric together, insert a chenille stick into the hole, leaving 22 cm protruding. Secure with hand-stitching to base of cone shape. Turn right side out and half-fill with lavender. Continue as for Lavender Sachet and bend top of chenille stick over to form an umbrella hook.

Note: All of these tree ornaments were designed by Mrs Anne Mayne of Newport, NSW.

LUXURY COATHANGERS

Made from your left-over fabrics, metal or wooden hangers and pretty trims, decorated coathangers are always a very welcome item at fêtes. They're both simple to sew and sensational to sell.

wire and wooden coathangers
thin wadding
small pieces of pretty fabric
laces
artificial flowers
ribbons

Lace Coathanger

1 Cut a rectangle of wadding 45 × 27 cm. Fold wadding around a wire hanger, pin then hand sew to secure.
2 Fold a 30 cm length of 1.5 cm-wide ribbon in half crossways wrong sides together. Sew along each 15 cm side. Slide tube of ribbon on hanger hook.
3 Cover hanger with satin or other suitable fabric as lining beneath lace. Fold 90 × 18 cm rectangle of lace in half, right sides together, and place padded hanger between layers. Pin along shaping of coat-hanger along top and sides. Slide hanger out and stitch fabric leaving hole for hook and lower edge open. Turn right side out; slip onto hanger. Sew a small running stitch across base of hanger cover to secure layers of lace together. Decorate with artificial flowers and a ribbon bow.

Satin Coathanger

1 Follow steps 1 and 2 as for Lace Coathanger.
2 Fold a 45 × 48 cm rectangle of satin crossways, right sides facing. Place under hanger. Mark line of shoulders and side sections leaving fabric extension below hanger. Stitch sides and shoulders leaving a small hole for hook at centre top and lower edge open. Turn right side out.
3 Gather an 80 cm-length of 6 cm-wide lace along top edge. Evenly spacing gathers along front lower edge of hanger cover and with right sides together, stitch in place. Fold hem along back under; slip stitch in place. Decorate hanger

Neat and Sweet Coathanger

Lace Coathanger

Ribboned Coathanger

Taffeta Coathanger

Satin Coathanger

with ribbons and an artificial flower.

Neat and Sweet Coathanger

1 Cut a strip 6 × 100 cm from thin wadding. Wrap around small wooden coathanger to pad; secure with hand stitching. Trim off excess wadding.
2 Cut two rectangles of print fabric each measuring 2 cm wider than hanger and 8 cm deep. Decorate right side of one rectangle with lace trim. Sew rectangles, right sides together, along sides and top, leaving a small opening for hook and lower edge open.

3 Attach 60 cm of 5 cm-wide lace to base following step 3 of Satin Coathanger. Slip stitch back to front at base. Decorate with satin ribbon.

Ribboned Coathanger

1 Prepare as for Neat and Sweet Coathanger, following Step 1.
2 Wrap hook with 1 m of 5 cm-wide satin ribbon. Cut off excess; stitch in place to secure at base of hook.
3 Fold 1.7 m of 10 cm-wide lace in half crossways. Stitch short end closed forming a 10 x 85 cm rectangle. Place hanger inside and using

a strong double thread, run a small gathering stitch by hand 5 mm inside top edge. Repeat along base close to hanger allowing excess lace to fall free. Draw gathers up evenly; secure with hand stitching. Decorate with ribbon.

Taffeta Coathanger

1 Construct in the same way as Ribboned Coathanger using pretty plain or patterned taffeta. Sew seams on inside and turn through to right side.
2 Follow step 3 of Satin Coathanger to attach lace to lower edge.